Fun on the Farm

Mary O'Keeffe

g **GILL** EDUCATION

pat

sit

tip

Welcome to Leahy's Farm!
This way ➡

4 Name the things in the picture that begin with k.

Look, trace and say

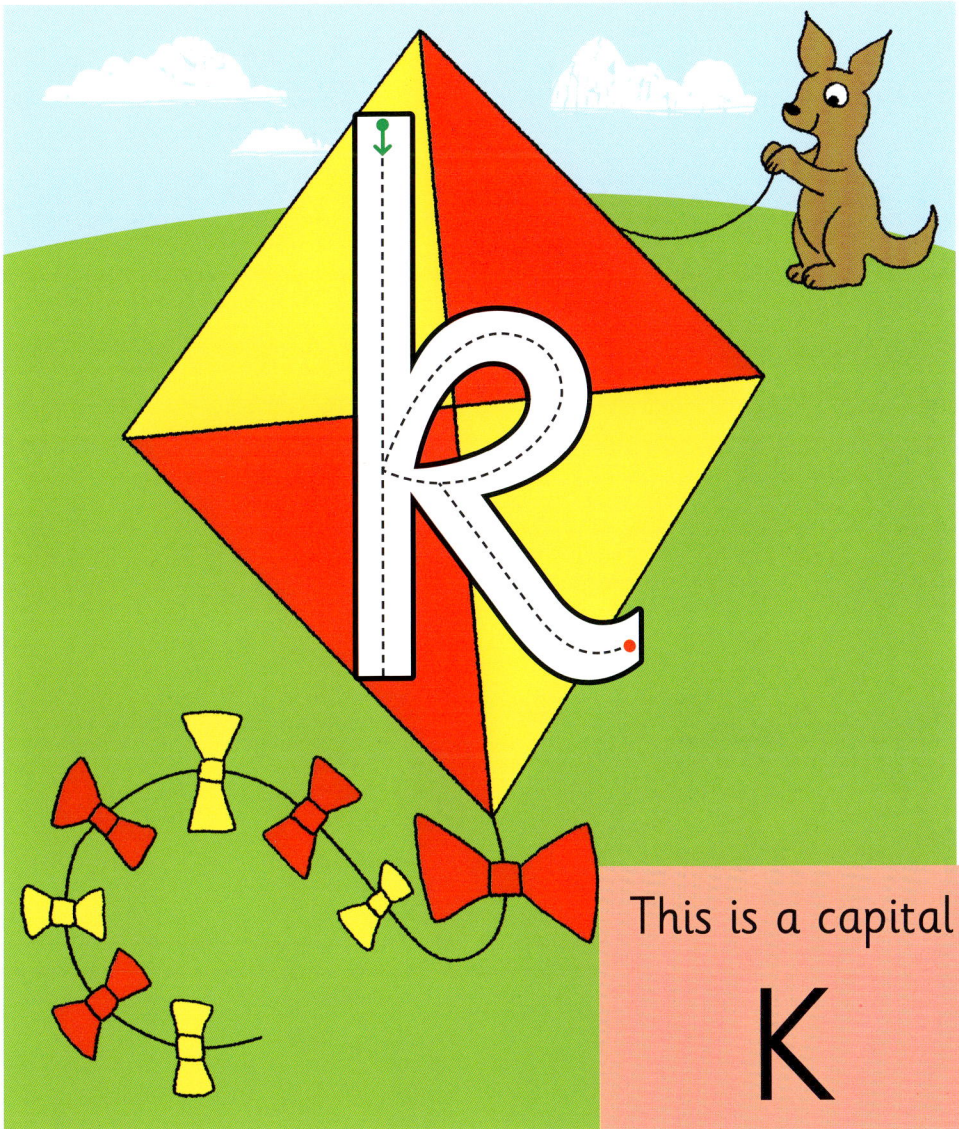

This is a capital

K

ENTER

EXIT

6 Name the things in the picture that begin with e.

Look, trace and say

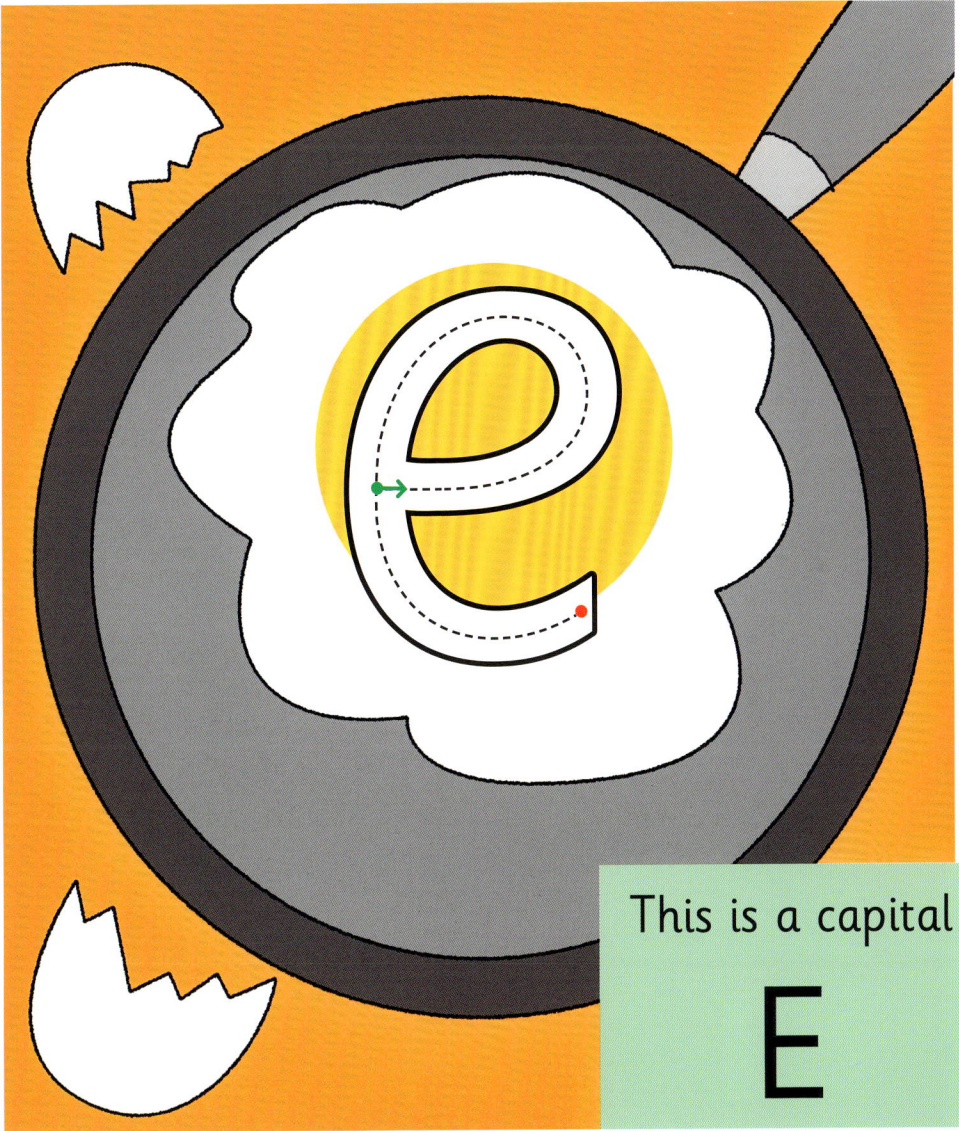

This is a capital

E

Name the things in the picture that begin with h.

Look, trace and say

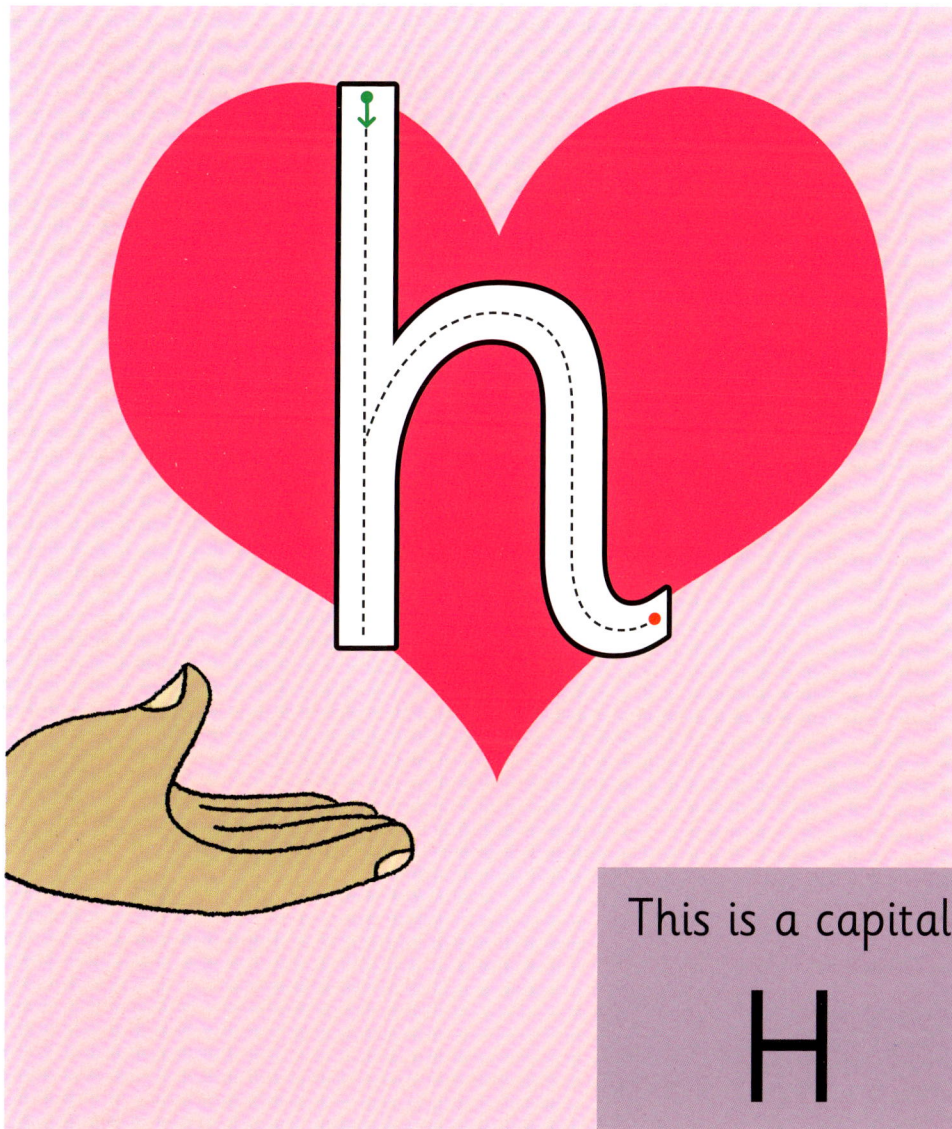

This is a capital

H

Name the things in the picture that begin with r.

Look, trace and say

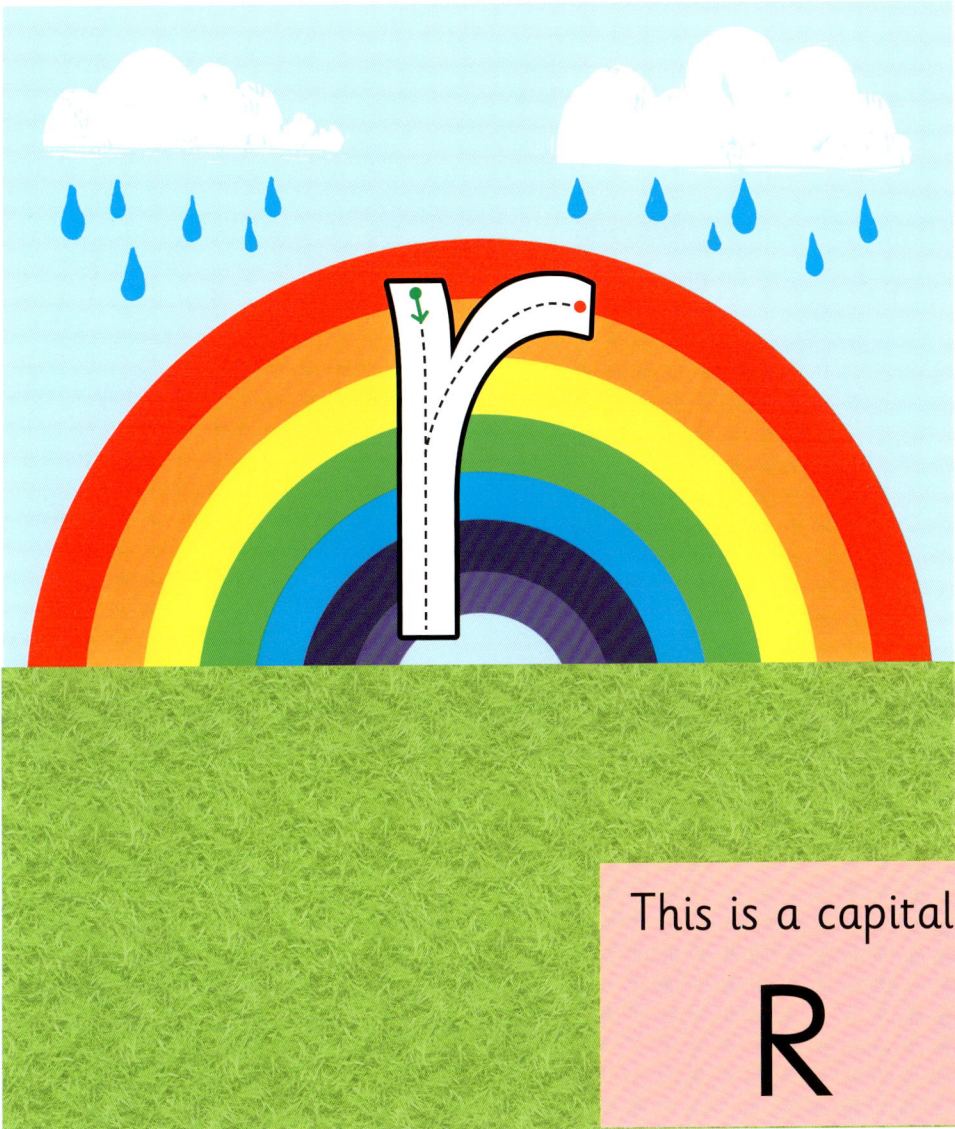

This is a capital

R

Name the things in the picture that begin with m.

Look, trace and say

This is a capital

M

nap

tap
tap!

I can look, trace and say

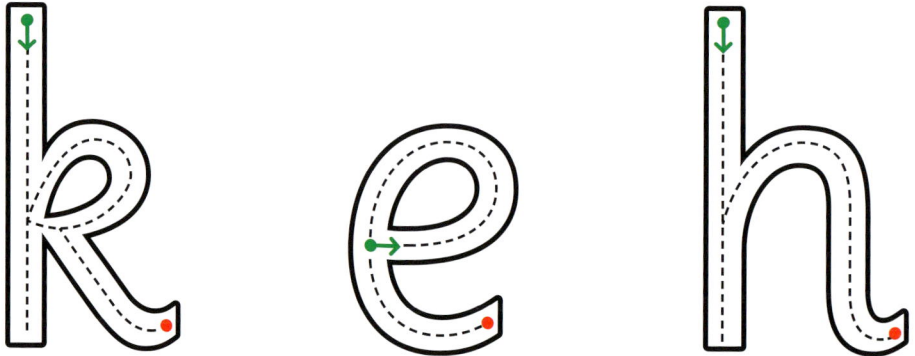

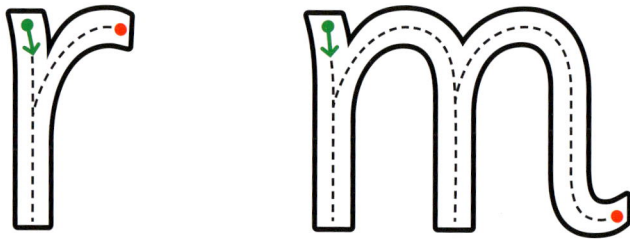

k e h

r m